Other Books by Dorothy Chan

Attack of the Fifty-Foot Centerfold

Revenge of the Asian Woman

BABE

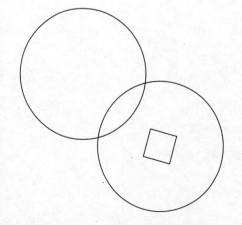

Our favorite Triple Sonnet Heroine does indeed reawaken our desires for "dishing" and "decadence" in *Return of the Chinese Femme*. In their latest dazzling collection, Dorothy K. Chan guides us through sumptuous frolic and feasting, from the "ideal relationship" beginning courtside at a Lakers game ("pass the hotdog") to Carmen Electra as " the superhero origin story of legends, or the starlet rising out of the clam shell" in a delicious set of "recipes" that all add up to a banquet of delights and dares ("give me some pearls—and fire"). Secret menus a little "sapphic" are shared with you, dear reader, where studmuffins "feed you strawberry cake in the bubble bath," post-constraints of "Victorian busts and Vanitas still lifes" which the poet bursts open with new energy, new meaning, new hungers. Never without humor, Chan takes on political and social inhibitions, turns them inside-out and upside-down, with a playfulness unique to the very mantra: "and oh, I crave and I crave and crave and crave." *Return of the Chinese Femme* won't leave you wanting, and yet wanting more from Chan, the next poem, the new collection which continues "K is for kink. K is for knot. K is for kissing,/K is for king. Crown me."
— **ROSEBUD BEN-ONI**, author of *If This Is the Age We End Discovery*

"I crave and I crave and crave and crave," writes Dorothy Chan in *Return of the Chinese Femme*. No contemporary poet craves in quite the same way. Chan's elegantly gargantuan appetite relishes everything from coconut and sago soup to Cantonese chicken wings; everything from "deviled eggs to mac and cheese, and Heart Attack Burgers on secret menus." Chan craves not only these litanies of dishes, but also sexual encounters with women and men, including those that "defy gender" – and always saves room to savor pop culture icons like Dennis Rodman and Rob Lowe (as Hello Kitty). From her "amuse-bouche" triple sonnets to her embedded recipes, Chan's work is delectably fiery. She moves between Asian and American cultures, as well as varied poetic forms, with finesse – and what (almost) rhymes with finesse? Fearless. That, for me, is the word to describe this book.
— **CHRISTINA PUGH**, author of *Stardust Media*

A juicy, fluffy, bouncy, and loud refusal of the mandate to enshrine the stereotype of the melancholic Asian prostate in the service of dominant understandings of our traumas. These poems are defiant in their exploration of the other side of hunger: the voracity and veracity of a femme's many appetites. Chan's verse is insatiably kinesthetic, persuasive in its strut, equally capable of evoking the exuberance of kinship and the scintillation of erotic connection. Because is it even a revolution if it does not romp? Please. Baby.
— **DIVYA VICTOR**, author of *CURB* and *KITH*

For Kristin and Lauren Chen — *"One of everything, please."*

Deep Vellum Publishing
3000 Commerce Street, Dallas,Texas 75226
deepvellum.org · @deepvellum

Deep Vellum is a 501c3 nonprofit literary arts organization founded in 2013
with the mission to bring the world into conversation through literature.

Support for this publication has been provided in part by grants from the National
Endowment for the Arts, the Texas Commission on the Arts, the City of Dallas Office
of Arts and Culture, the Communities Foundation of Texas, and the Addy Foundation.

Paperback ISBN: 9781646053100
Ebook ISBN: 9781646053254

Library of Congress Cataloging-in-Publication Data

Names: Chan, Dorothy (Dorothy Ka-Ying), author.
Title: Return of the Chinese femme : poems / Dorothy Chan.
Description: First edition. | Dallas, Texas : Deep Vellum, 2024.
Identifiers: LCCN 2023048751 (print) | LCCN 2023048752 (ebook) | ISBN
    9781646053100 (trade paperback) | ISBN 9781646053254 (ebook)
Subjects: LCGFT: Poetry.
Classification: LCC PS3603.H35565 R48 2024 (print) | LCC PS3603.H35565
    (ebook) | DDC 811/.6--dc23/eng/20231025
LC record available at https://lccn.loc.gov/2023048751
LC ebook record available at https://lccn.loc.gov/2023048752

Cover photo: *Your Inheritance* by Grace Sydney Pham
Cover art and design by Christina Vang, La Bang Studio
Interior layout and typesetting by Christina Vang, La Bang Studio

PRINTED IN CANADA

RETURN OF THE CHINESE FEMME

DOROTHY CHAN

RETURN OF THE CHINESE FEMME

Poems

Dorothy Chan

THIS EVENING'S MENU:
A TABLE OF CONTENTS

III. The Recipes for Disaster, Sex, and Popular Culture

IV. An Ode to Decadence

V. One More Dessert for Discovery

I.
RECIPE FOR AN ASIAN FEMME: I'M A SNACK; I'M A TEASE; I'M THE DISH.

Ode to Chinese Superstitions, Haircuts, and Being a Girl

Chinese superstition tells me it's bad luck
         to get a haircut when I'm sick, and my hair
gets cut twice a year, because I let it grow,
         tying it into a ponytail, exposing my forehead
looking like I'm the protagonist of an anime,
         which makes me think about my last name,
Chan, also known as the Japanese honorific
         for someone endearing. Chan, like a friend

                              or someone childlike. I've been told I sound
                    like a child when I pick up the phone, or maybe
                              it's my pure joy to hear from the ones I love.
                    And yes, voices are sexier than faces, so dial me,
                              honey, let's get a little wild tonight, as I pour
                    a glass of bourbon and picture myself in anime—
                              cartoon Chan starring in a slice-of-life show
                    about a girl group trying to make it, and you bet

I'd be the rambunctious one, the tomboy-
         rabble-rouser-ringleader on the drums—
the trouble with the exposed forehead, also
         known in East Asian culture as a symbol
of aggression, because an exposed forehead
         puts everything out there—you're telling
the world you're ready for a takedown,
         and according to my father, good Chinese

                              girls never show their foreheads, and I know
                    he wishes I were born in the Year of the Rabbit,
                              like my mother, the perfect woman with flawless
                    skin who never causes trouble with the boys, but
                              no, I'm the Year of the Snake, and I always bring
                    the party, cause the trouble, or as my lover says,
                              I'm sarcastic wit personified, and it's boundless,
                    because I am Dorothy—pop embodied in a gingham

skirt with a puppy and a picnic basket
        filled with prosciutto and gouda and Prosecco,
but really, what *is* my fate? And my mother
        tells me the family fortune teller got me all
wrong, because there's no way in hell
        I'd end up being a housewife with three
children and breadwinner of a husband.
        But of course, the fortune teller got my brother's

                        fate right. It's moments like this when I wonder
            if I even matter because I'm a girl and not a boy.
                It's moments like this when I think about my fate,
            or how Chinese superstition tells me not to cut or wash
                my hair on Lunar New Year, so all my good fortune
            won't be snipped away. But really, what is fate?
                I tie my hair back and put on a short skirt, ready
            to take over the world—forehead forever exposed.

Triple Sonnet for Silver Foxes, Dear Dad, and Alex Trebek,
                                   Teach Me Something Actually Useful

Because I've inherited my mother's face,
            I worry I've inherited her taste in men,
and why did I play Lolita in my twenties,
            tugging at the heartstrings of silver foxes
whose wives left them the weekend before,
            and don't you dare ask me how a woman plays
Lolita at twenty-two, because *this* is power,
            baby, lollipop in my mouth, red lips and even
redder cheeks, eye fucking silver foxes straight
            out of Carrie Bradshaw's date-of-the-week-
politician-style-fantasy on *Sex and the City,*
            silver foxes who bought me Whiskey Sours
and Mai Tais, because every girl goes through
            a sweet drinks phase in college,

            and I'd like an Amaretto Sour with Luxardo
cherries now, and take a shot with me,
            I don't have daddy issues, but Dear Dad,
I'll never forgive you for dating Mom when
            she turned eighteen, when you were a grown-
ass-thirty-two-year-old man who should've
            known better, and What is Ephebophilia?
should really be a question, no, a *category*
            on *Jeopardy,* and Alex, I'll take that for $1000,
because I'm an expert for life, and I've never
            watched your show, because know-it-all white
boys flaunting useless information is a turnoff.
            Alex, teach me something useful, like how to
make sense of my mother's and father's history

in Hong Kong, and I want to punch my own
            father in the face, in 2019, when he proudly says
he dated my mother because he needed someone
            to take care of his two boys, as if the sole purpose

of women on earth is to nurse men, as if

        the sole purpose of women on earth is to

cook your favorite soups and scrub the floors

        until you can see your own damn reflection,

and Alex Trebek, What is Ephebophilia?

        I don't trust you to teach me something

actually useful. And sometimes, I wish

        I built a time machine to stop my mother

from signing on to a life with my father,

        but where would that leave me, where would it.

Triple Sonnet for Veronica Lodge's Tigers

There are too many poems about fathers.
Or not enough. I used to hate mine until
        I remembered the fortune teller's theory
that my father and I are symbols of each
        other—maybe this is why in my dreams
I say goodbye to him last whenever
        I go on a mission across the river—We're
a Tiger Father and a Snake Daughter who
        aren't supposed to get along, the insistence
of tigers that they're the leaders of the zodiac—
        the secrecy of snakes, like how the idea of
living a discreet life resonates so much with
        queer little me. A lover asks if my father
knows that I've kissed girls. I tell him that

men don't need to know everything. Tiger Dads
        always do the most—or is the magical four
letter word actually best in this case. As a child,
        I took home the gold from math competitions:
use the four numbers on the card to create 24—
        I'd watch other children cry when they lost
their rounds, stoic little me staring at their tears,
        their mothers hugging them, saying they could
now leave and go to McDonald's. How sad it is
        to lose and eat McNuggets, is a feeling I'll never
know, because my dad was always the last person
        I said goodbye to before rounds—my lucky symbol,
two rivers cross—I don't want to get all Freud,
        but my mother and I get along better in life,

while my father and I get along better in dreams,
both real and imagined. In Kowloon, he takes me
        to the McDonald's where he won a gold pen
when he was a young man. Tiger Dads only breed
        winners, and more stories where I inherit qualities

from my dad: his high alcohol tolerance, his habit

     of four hours of sleep per night, the assumption of

authority everywhere I go—the raw ambition,

     and I feel like Veronica Lodge in the episode

when she visits the guidance counselor who tells her

     that Veronica and her father are parallels of each

other. Like Veronica, I'm the desirable girl walking

     around like I own the place, whose father would buy

me a baby tiger if he could—pushing me to win at life.

Designer

Like Flavor Flav taking Sweetie to Red Lobster on their first date, during the first season of Flavor of Love.

I forget his order. But I learned how happiness comes in small things. I think about seafood tanks in Hong Kong restaurants. How summers ago, at Dim Sum, my grandpa and I watched the tanks together. How the abalone and inches of prawns and lobsters with whiskers and big-lipped-injected fish floated. How summers ago, Grandpa told me he wanted more poems about eels. How he predicted the future. What Chinese Grandpa isn't magical. As a three-year-old in Kowloon, I dreaded seafood market trips—the eels jutting their heads out, their midnight tails wrapping around each other, their tiny teeth sticking out of the tank. How I knew one would slip out and eat three-year-old me holding a mango soft serve. Their orgy. How the eel is the sexier, electric version of the femme born in the Year of the Snake. Fate. How Grandpa predicted the future. What Chinese Grandpa isn't magical. I think about snake patched jackets walking down Gucci runways. I think about how twenty-three-year-old me once dated a twice-my-age-you-do-the-math-Singaporean-fashion-designer-who-once-dressed-presidents-past-his-prime. How summers ago, he gifted me a pink snakeskin handbag. How summers ago, his older sister forbade me from ever seeing him again. You do the math. It's still fashion. I think about seafood tanks in Hong Kong restaurants—how my grandpa is waiting for me, ordering the abalone.

So Chinese Girl

Anyone who makes tasty food has to be a good person,
        because think about all the love that goes into cooking:
salt and pepper, sprinkle a little extra cheese, and pop open

        a bottle of Syrah, or if we're eating at my parents'
in Las Vegas, we're drinking Tsingtao beer, my father's favorite,
        and he adds more bamboo shoots and straw mushrooms

and baby corn, and fun fact: when I was a baby, I'd only
        eat corn and carrot-flavored mush, and now, my dad adds
more to the Buddha's Delight, a vegetarian dish from China,

        and I think about my aunt in Hong Kong, who once
a year, buys fish from restaurants, only to release them
        back into the sea—eat tofu—save a life—but back to dinner

in Vegas, my mom is making her Cantonese lobster, extra
        garlic and ginger, and I grew up licking lobster shells
for their sauce, I grew up waking up during summer

        vacations to my mother wearing a headband, warding off
grease from cooking crabs and shrimps, heads intact,
        and there's something, just *something* about my parents'

cooking that makes me feel a little more Chinese girl,
        because I don't live in Hong Kong, and unlike my cousins,
my daily stop isn't Bowring Street station where I could pick up

        fresh mango cake before it's sold out, or what about
chocolate mousse cake in the shape of a bunny or dome
        cakes shaped like cows and pigs or cakes shaped like

watermelons and shikuwasa and citrus mikans, and who wouldn't
        want custard egg tarts or hot dogs wrapped in sweet bread or
sesame balls, washing it all down with cream soda, and I feel

like that little Chinese Girl in Kowloon again, getting
picked up by my grandpa after preschool, ready to go junk
        shopping, and I'd come home with shrimp crackers and a toy

turtle aquarium and a snowman painting and a dozen roses,
        and no, I don't even like flowers anymore, but there's
something, just *something* about thrifting with my grandpa

        now at age twenty-eight that makes me feel so Chinese Girl,
the way he bargains in the stalls, asking for the best, "How much
        for that Murakami-era Louis Vuitton" or "What about this vintage

Armani?" and it's like that look he gives me at dim sum, after
        the sampler platter of shumai and har gow and chicken feet
and char siu bao comes, and he tells me to eat everything,

        watching me chow down on Chinese ravioli, and that face of his
freezes in the moment, "Eat more, eat more, eat more. Are you
        happy?" And oh, Grandpa, I'm so happy I could eat forever.

Ode to Heavy Appetizers and Many Big Loves

"The dish would like two dishes," he says,
        and I'm reminded of the time the composer
asked me if I wanted to take a Sunday ride
        in his vintage Thunderbird—a scene straight
out of the America I don't live in, whereas
        I'm stuck in the universe where I can't make up
my mind when it comes to love. T tells me,
        "If you think you're non-monogamous,"

                protect that with all your heart, because everyone
      will want you all to themselves," and what will be
           left for me? My lobster-stuffed salmon and clams
in white wine come, and he hands me his martini—
           sharing is caring, and let's talk about appetites,
      or how the heiress on television says she loves when
           a man works with his hands, and I feel you, babe,
I love when a man works me with his hands,

or let's call it the Holy Grail of chemistry
        or the Chemical X of sugar and spice
and everything musky and a voice that's
        husky yet soft touching my body, and oh,
isn't he so cute? I blush like I'm a sixteen-
        year-old-girl again, writing in my diary:
Some men are good for both transportation
        and kissing—that little tingle of pleasure,

            or the face a lover makes when we reconnect:
      heart eyes emoji, heart eyes emoji, heart eyes emoji,
           and *What does it mean to fall in love?* I wonder,
then remember how *F* once told me I'd have
        many great loves in my life, if the five lines
underneath my left pinky are any indication, or
        it's what T says, "I'm starting to believe there's
many great loves and not just one." I tell her,

"I think it's different for women," like how
          Dona Flor had two husbands, one for orgasm
and one for public appearances, and what's more
          important, the bed or the desk? Or that spectral
fantasy when the first husband, a ghost, enters her
          and no one else can see him, and I think we all
have secret lives—the moments when the mirror's
          right above us, while we make love, and we watch

                              ourselves. I think about how *The New York Times*
                    told us to ask each other thirty-six questions and then
                              fall in love, gazing into each other's eyes. Given
                    the choice of anyone in the world, I'd have Dracula
                              over as a dinner guest. Every future love already
                    thinks I'm a freak. We'd dine on heavy appetizers:
                              mini sliders, Crab Rangoon, and beer cheese.
                    One night, I tell a lover to be my tease forever.

She Asks Me What I Want in a Life Partner

And I know we'll never work the minute I tell her

> I want someone to take over the world with, which
> sounds like the theme to *Pinky and the Brain*.

But my future and I would both be Brain—two
attention whores playing the mouse genius

> who invented the Internet, also known as ultimate
> world domination, and twice is nicer anyway,

like the Las Vegas Strip's New York New York
Hotel and Casino slogan: "The city so vice

> they named it twice," and everyone wants a woman
> who's both brains and beauty, but it's much

more complicated than the 130+ IQ and overlined red
lips—it's about walking into the room like you're

> the most important person. But I'm tired of being
> objectified. I want my cake. I want to eat it too.

I want to be king because I defy gender. Handsome
men in suits are the most tiring people on earth

> because they're trying too hard or not enough.
> I'll be your little art monster, the cyclops awakening

during the midnight romp, and you know it's time
to take over the world with our wits and wiles—

> always femme, my dear, and wild wild wild wild.

Triple Sonnet for Dennis Rodman, #91, on my Television Screen

       I tell R that McDonald's has sold out of
the special $6 celebrity rapper meal,
       and it's a moment straight out of my nineties
childhood when Michael Jordan had his own
       burger: the McJordan with smoked bacon, cheese,
and BBQ sauce, and don't forget the onions,
       and don't you wish your beloved would call you
nicknames like McGorgeous or McLovely
       or at least McPretty, and I wonder if names
like that are reserved for run-of-the-mill white
       guy doctors/actors on television shows past their
prime. All I know is I'm mad my meal is sold
       out. All I know is Dennis Rodman was my favorite
Bulls player as a kid, and how I remember

              his green hair on the court or what about when
he dyed it yellow with leopard spots or the time
              it was a smiley face in the back, and he really was
a performer, even a dancer. And who could forget
              when he declared he was going to marry himself,
showing up to Barnes and Noble in a wedding dress
              and a parade of bifauxnen behind him. Cheers to you,
Dennis, and thank you for giving me a childhood:
              January 2, 1998 when you hit three three pointers
in a row. Give me a triple triple. At fast food joints
              everyone asks for a double double, but why ask
for two when you could have three, and we all know
              thrice is even nicer, like how Spumoni ice cream
isn't complete without cherry, and Neapolitan

isn't anything without strawberry, and have
       you tried the astronaut version that's one
hard block? But who wants it dry when
       you could be wet is a rhetorical question
for every context. Give me a triple espresso

with a Triple Decker Dagwood with olive
on top, and oh, Dagwood, you lucky fool,
　　how did you ever score a babe like Blondie?
Count your blessings. Give me a juicy pickle
　　from the largest glass jar. Appetizer.
Entrée. Dessert. The rule of three applies
　　to meals the most. Or I'll take a triple topping
pizza: anchovies, sausage, and olives, throw
　　in a soda to wash it all down—three wishes.

II.
THE TRIPLE SONNETS: CLASSIC AMUSE-BOUCHES WITH A TWIST

Triple Sonnet for Black Hair

My mother warns me not to blow-dry my hair
      too hard, turning it from black to rust, and
I must wear my black hair proudly. Black,
      the color of clothing my grandmother hates,
because young women should always wear red
      or pink, the colors of luck and youth. Black,
the color of wedding dress the reality TV
      starlet, circa 2006 wants, but she knows
walking down the aisle in black will break
      her mother's heart, and fact: red is the color
of wedding dresses in Chinese culture—even
      if the bride wears white for the ceremony,
she'll change into red for the dinner—hello,
      ten course meal of my dreams that starts

      with a meat platter of roasted pork, and how
guests go crazy for the abalone and swallow's
      nest soup with crab meat, and of course there's
a chicken, a pig, a fish, a duck, and a lobster—
      roll call. And fact: at Chinese funerals, relatives
of the deceased don't wear black, but white.
      And fact: eight's the lucky Chinese number,
not seven, and at dim sum, my grandmother
      makes sure she orders eight dishes, not seven,
but nine's alright too. Eight, like the number of
      legs on a spider—a spider, black, like my hair
that my mother warns me not to blow-dry
      too hard, turning it into rust, and I remember
my sixth-grade science experiment of lighting

a cigarette, watching how the smoke changed
      the spider's web spinning. And black, because
it's hypnotic, like little black dresses on gorgeous
      women, or how I prefer my lingerie in black
over white, but red is probably the best, an ode

to sexiness—an ode to the color of my culture
and history, and I want to feel like a million
dollars—be a million dollars. And black, the color
of my late dog, Buzzie, a Skye Terrier, twice as long
as he was low, my mother once joking he looked
like a giant rat. Or a licorice bunny. Or a furry snake.
Or a dragon in some iterations of love, majestic in
dreams—how I miss him after these dream visits,
black, the color of my wet hair in the morning.

Triple Sonnet for Corn Soup

My friend Rita jokes that all Asians love corn,
        and I wonder if there's ever been a study
conducted, a correlation the way five-star
        restaurants in Hong Kong always begin meals
with corn soup then oysters then steak and lobster,
        and why, oh why, do we keep aiming for western
civilization like it's the height of all sophistication,
        and keep your surf and turf, because my lobster
needs a little ginger, a little garlic and soy sauce,
        and look at this Cantonese corn soup right in front
of us, ready to be devoured in its egg-droppy
        goodness, and hello, I'm reminded of childhood
summer mornings of my mother cooking this soup
        that's been in our family for centuries and centuries—

        Take chicken stock and eggs and half a teaspoon
of sesame oil and salt and pepper, and oh,
        creamed corn, and taste the most delicious
soup in the world that my mother remembers
        from her childhood of Grandpa coming home
with knockoff watches and dolls with glass eyes
        after work overseas, and how he'd start cooking,
while my mother and her sisters and brother
        played with these life-size dolls in an apartment
in Kowloon the size of a rich person's
        walk-in closet, and that right there was all
the happiness in the world, of a home-cooked meal,
        of clouds of egg whites my mother tasted
light and fluffy in this mixture of corn,

and when I was a baby, the only mush I'd eat
        was carrot or corn flavored, spitting out anything
else or giving stank face to my parents,
        and when I was four, in Kowloon, Grandpa
picked me up from school, took me shopping,

buying me corn-flavored puff munchies,
while we looked at snowman paintings
         and toy turtle aquariums, and a fishing game—
sink the rod, capture the rainbow fish,
         and oh, how Grandpa bought me everything,
then off to the grocery store we went
         for creamed corn—at checkout, me eating
snowball-shaped mochi ice cream, and no,
         I wasn't too full for the greatest soup in the world.

Triple Sonnet for Dragons Spitting Out Pearls

My best friend's fish is pregnant again,
and I think about my aunt in Hong Kong
who releases fish back into the ocean
once a year, buying them from restaurants
boasting their seafood in tanks—feng shui,
because if your restaurant's got one arowana,
translated from Chinese as "the dragon fish
spits out the pearl," it'll do fine, but with two,
pearls and pearls will rain down your meals,
getting caught in oysters and abalone and lobster,
and isn't seafood so beautiful in this greatest
music video of all time starring your arowana,
oh arowana, you dimepiece of a fish, let me
write odes for you, how you inspire

black market bad boys and girls, and calling
all supervillains, it's time to unite, don
those eyepatches, because the arowana
can be trained like a cat or a dog
by your side, and though it's caged
in a tank, it's a dragon—a damn dragon
that'll let you take over the world,
breathing fire, spitting out pearls,
and my aunt stares at tanks of seafood
in Kowloon, and of course, she can't afford
an arowana, a six-digit-cost-display-
inside-like-a-Manet-painting-on-a-gilded-
gold-plane, so she buys regular fish citizens,
releasing them back into water,

giving new meaning to spa days of fish
eating away at your dead skin—the Buddhist
lifestyle of giving back, and oh, how I wish
my best friend's gold fish was pregnant
with an arowana—maybe mommy goldfish

could first grow fifty times its size,
        a superhero giving birth to a supervillain,
and yes, I know it's impossible, but just
        just imagine those pearls and pearls raining
on enough meals to feed everyone
        in Hong Kong, and I think about all the little
boys and girls staring at tanks outside
        of restaurants, trying to grab onto a lobster tail—
the adventure—give me some pearls—and fire.

Designer

Like Rob Lowe on Thanksgiving chowing down on a plate of hot wings too spicy for his white-boy-heartthrob-spanning-decades-your-mom-liked-him-too tastes. Like the first hot sauce that's already too hot for him to handle. A metaphor. Because girl, a boy may be hot, but if he can't handle the hotness, that's 10 points off and a shove out the door. Do not pass go. Do not collect $200. Do not double text me ever again. Because if he can't handle spice, how's he going to handle sugar. Who freaks out at a one? Who cares if he ages like Hello Kitty—timeless—big in the '80s, but a refined whiskey now, or both vintage and fresh like the best designer. Not worth the price tag. Designer, like when Hello Kitty strutted down the runway in the early aughts to Heatherette's (RIP) celebutante fashion show. How East Asian girls grow up with Hello Kitty. How East Asian girls grow old with Hello Kitty. How sugar and spice and everything nice and Chemical X leads to femme power—pass me that plate of wings—I remember attending an all boys' party in the 2000s chowing down a plate of Buffalo's spiciest—photos of me downing milk afterwards—don't let that resurface on the Internet. My throat full of spices. The hotness covering my magenta mouth—designer lipstick makes the world go round and round.

Designer

Like a drug. A power femme with an Ivy League degree. The mini handbag she carries, containing one stick of gum, one condom, one pen, and a credit card, though cash is the easiest getaway. Leave the twenty, and let's run, baby. Once, a man at the Cornell bookstore asked nineteen-year-old me what brand of handbag he could buy me. Miu Miu. Me Me. I hate it when rich white men call women materialistic. She's after your money? Hand it over now. Please.

Please. The word lovers should say more. Please RSVP. Please put on the blindfold now. Please may I come in and shut the door and give you the best head of your life tonight. Please. Baby. I'll slip off my pink panties. Please, as in short for pleasure, as in what Charlotte York, before she was York-Goldenblatt, denied in the episode when the power lesbians came hungry for art, and she was tired of men, in her designer. Prada loafers. Designer, like the lesbian Queen Bee with her Athena sculpture in the foyer saying to "sweetheart" Charlotte, "...if you're not going to eat pussy, you're not a dyke." And Charlotte, Honey, no, you didn't earn a seat at this table. Take your designer loafers and go home.

Designer, like the tablecloth we magic trick off before fucking on the table. I think of this dream: the centerpieces of lemons and glassware and China stocked with the finest matcha cakes filled with red bean, from Japan, sliding off, you sliding into me—like a Baroque painting reborn.

Triple Sonnet for Celebrities with Three Names

If you've got three names and you're famous
does that mean three times the amount of fucking?
        I daydream about my ideal lovers and hearing
Cut! when the director tells us to switch positions
        on the set of our bedroom, and what's a bigger
turn-on than someone saying your name under
        the covers—how about saying your name three
times, and oh, *fuck, fucking, fuckest*—yeah that's
        a superlative, like the Beetlejuice effect, only
freakier, like let's get transported into the house
        I built in a simulation game where my avatar
seduced then killed the richest man for the sake
        of inheriting then remodeling his mansion into
her dream of glass windows in every room—

the pleasure of always watching what's going
        on, and I swear, I'm a really nice girl. I really
am. Just say the magic word, and I'm all yours,
        and surveys reveal that the word lovers wished
their lovers said more is "please," and I wonder
        if please is short for pleasure, as in eat your girl
right, as in I'll order a clitty clitty bang bang at
        a midnight viewing, as in please let me put on
a show for you, as in I love any event with a ton
        of cameras, as in keep feeding me macarons
while you're feeling me up in the bath, and if
        I was a celebrity, I'd tack my middle initial
K back into my name for extra effect, my secret

        K, as in Ka-Ying, as in white boys will you
stop calling me by my middle name because
        you think speaking Cantonese will bring us
closer, and it's ironic how an actual lover
        adds in the K every time she says my full

name, and she says it with such authority it's

       a turn-on, like, *Baby, say my full name again*

and I'll record you, why don't you, K?

       K is for kink. K is for knot. K is for kissing,

K is for king. Crown me. And don't fool me

       by saying Queen, because I know where all

my power lies. And K is for knock me down

       and pin me down on the grass, lover, because

you on me is the closest to nature I'm ever getting.

Chinese Girl Strikes Back

I know what I'm getting myself into
        when he's naked in bed, and I'm doodling
bears, bows, speech balloons, and bunnies
        on the hotel notepad, because I'm a 5'4"
Chinese girl with a baby face and a chest
        that keeps growing, so I might as well keep
the image up—my superpower, my seduction—
        my forever line of telling strangers that I don't
like to dance, but I do like to grind on men, then
        run away, or how I always look oh so innocent
no matter what I'm doing, like right now,
        as I'm plastering my hotel masterpieces
all over his chiseled body, and damn boy,
        I want to take a picture, eat you up, rub you

                all over, but actually, I don't, and I think about
            what my friend Adam says about power—the ways
                I have it, the way I can tell that this man I'm with
            in this hotel room has Yellow Fever—Asian Fetish—
                whatever you want to call the whole nine yards or
            Everything But the Kitchen Sink Sundae of wanting
                the Eastern Other—the Woman with Cat Eyes
            and black silky hair, as lover, and I feel like a femme
                fatale. And I really should run, but as Adam says,
            and I know all too well, I love how this man doesn't
                know that I know about his case of Yellow Fever,
            and I'm sure his bros have it too—his Achille's Heel—
                his googly eyes at my round face and lips acting like
            I could chop something off any minute, and I remember

the plastic carrot and turnip toys with knife
        I had as a kid, chopping each section of fake
vegetable off, but really, there's a beauty in
        this mystery of him not knowing that I know.
It's a hidden superpower, I say to Kristin and Alex

in San Francisco, after Alex says his superpower
is blending in, and of course, we're not talking about
        powers like strength or invisibility or flight or talking
to fish or x-ray vision, which is a damn shame, because
        I'd take x-ray vision any day, but I guess, back in
the hotel room, I don't even need it, as this man
        is naked in bed while I'm doodling, and I'm that
Chinese girl who strikes back—running away once
        I'm done chopping off your most prized possession.

Triple Sonnet for Asian Girlfriends: Cancel My Membership

The Asian Girlfriends of White Guys Club
is a membership I never want to renew,
        so cancel my card—I need space in my Juicy
Couture wallet, and according to dating sites,
        girls who look like me get the most action,
but what else is new when some dude's grand-
        dad regaled him with tales that Asian girls
are more fuckable with their tight pussies,
        the sideways-vagina-Holy-Grail-of-breakfast-
specials, and old men, stop with your war stories,
        get away from my tight ass pussy—let me protect
her with the world's finest lingerie, and I pose
        in front of the mirror, snapping photos the way
painters used to eye fuck their muses, but I'm

                my own damn muse, thank you very much,
                        and I crave seduction, remembering how
                I played Aphrodite in an elementary school
                        play—how I bemoaned that role, because
                What's up with the Goddess of Love and Ares?
                        Who would be attracted to war, to rage, to incest,
                and why does every girl end up with either angry
                        guy Ares or ugly guy Hephaestus when she's
                the prize herself, and Vanna White, let me spin
                        the wheel again, or whatever game show it is
                when I can choose another door, and where's
                        my golden Dalmatian or my endless supply
                of cotton candy ice cream or my vacation to
                        Tokyo, and you bet your ass, I'm taking a friend,

        not a lover, because what is love—and you've
hurt me once more. And you've hurt me once
        more. No, I don't want ni hao. I don't want
masculine hands on my thigh. I don't want
        a masculine hand holding my hand. A ten inch

height difference is only cute for a month.

      After that, my neck hurts trying to hug you.
I don't want a spork when we're eating dim

      sum. I don't want iced water when we're eating
dim sum. Get your hands off my char siu bao.

      Like, are you actually cute or are western dating
standards telling me you're the ideal man—

      the Adonis to my Asian Aphrodite, and wait,
I've got the myth wrong. But who really cares.

Triple Sonnet and Three Cheers for the Asian Bachelorette

Yena wants an Asian Bachelorette,
        but she's worried our Bachelorette
will get disowned by her family,
        because nothing screams *Dear Mom and Dad*
abandon me more than a starring role
        on reality TV and even the thought
of casual dating, and I wonder why
        parents like mine expect me to pop out
a baby when I wasn't supposed to date
        in my twenties. It's like the stork flew in,
and out came the perfect black-haired child
        I'd dedicate my life to, giving up poetry,
along with the endless cycle of girls and
        boys and great lovers in infatuation,

              and my problem is that I can't say yes,
        though I think *yes, done,* and *one* are
              the sexiest words in the English language,
        or maybe *I'm* the Asian Bachelorette
              Yena so desires—the female lead who
        leaves you hanging each week because
              I can't make up my mind when it comes
        to love. I'll cry on cue in a ballroom gown
              in a castle in Switzerland, after a tough
        elimination, regretting my decision right
              away, but scratch that, I'd never wear
        an evening dress since I hate formal wear,
              and nothing turns me off more than a man
        in a suit, and why all the focus on the outfits

when this is my life and my feelings
        and the hot sex I crave every night
under the covers, and what if I played
        my *Bachelorette* role more *Flavor of Love*
or *I Love New York,* giving out nicknames

to pass the time, because we all need
a little levity when it comes to love,
                so how's about *Stud* or *8-Pack* or *Sailor
Uranus* to my Sailor Neptune. And yes
                to all this cheer especially when the final two
meet my family over hotpot, and I end up
                choosing the one they dislike, but scratch that,
I'll eliminate both, because nothing's better
                than being a free agent who doesn't settle.

III.
THE RECIPES FOR DISASTER, SEX, AND POPULAR CULTURE

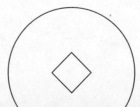

I'm the Sad Girl in the Anime Masturbating

on the phone to the lover she didn't choose,

       rubbing my clit to his sounds while looking
       at photos of younger, hotter men

with dimples and sly smiles. I try to convince
myself I could love him, because when someone

       older and in power tells you you work too much
       and should settle down and learn to cook

cordon bleu and buy more furniture, you listen,
or I'm convinced the o in love stands for obligation,

       as in I'm supposed to be over the moon and stars
       and sun for the "love" he's so "selflessly"

offering me. *O* stands for we own each other,
as in "I'm the only one for you," he says,

       and "Don't tell me about the last man you had
       sex with, because my feelings will be hurt,"

and "I look forward to sharing more beautiful
words with a beautiful woman," he writes me

       in a card, and oh, *O* is my mouth wanting to
       throw up. *O*, my face craving to orgasm

tonight, while tuning out his voice and looking
at actual hunks, as he tries to convince me

       he's handsome by name dropping Jim Carrey
       and Robert Downey Jr. and even John

Malkovich, as his celebrity doppelgängers
at various stages of his life, and I blame myself,

        wondering how and why I always wind up in
        situations where I can't escape, like when he

trapped me in a hotel room in Florida, not letting
go of me in bed, until I kissed him back:

        a man in his forties going after a pretty Asian
        girl, and is that all I am, I wonder, rubbing

peach lotion on my legs, breathing a sigh
of relief, because I can't think of a single

        look-alike for myself, and I don't like how
        his voice travels at one hundred words a minute,

like I'm seated at an auction, but he's the one
bidding on me. Maybe I like being the prize

        but hate being taken home by a strange man
        who buys too many antiques and overpriced

paintings. I wonder how monogamy ever worked
for anyone, or if we're all just stuck in the infinite

        cycle of lovers we hate, since timing is the worst
        and best part of existence. I mute him, then spread

my legs wide open O, and take a photo for another
man, now asleep, because I know he'll love a good

        morning surprise, that sexiness and safety of this
        man I crave, picturing him holding me tighter.

Recipe for Rudeness

I ask my parents how they feel about having
        100% purebred Chinese grandkids at their age,
at the dinner table, when my brother's home
        for New Year's, showing off his perfect
Cantonese girlfriend who doesn't speak
        a word of Cantonese, who isn't dining with us
because she's at a five-star restaurant
        in Hong Kong after flying business class

when she's not on business, and I add more beef
        to the hotpot, more enoki, more shrimp, less hate,
but I can't help myself when my brother hasn't
        been home in five years, didn't visit my father
during his heart attack, and poof, now he thinks
        this fourth-date marriage to a *good Chinese girl*
solves everything—the promise of family legacy,
        but nope, I hate to break it to you, brother, but

Chan is about *the* most common name in all of
        China, and we aren't rich or bluebloods, so what
are you even talking about with legacy, marrying
        a woman you met three months ago, and I drink
more Tsingtao, get a little sad while my brother
        adds more scallops and squid in the hotpot just
for me and he smiles and then coughs from
        the gochujang, the Korean hot pepper paste

and so do my mother and father, and I think about
        endurance, how I hide my boyfriends from my father
who wants 100% purebred Cantonese babies
        out of me, but no one controls my body, *no one—*
how nine years ago at a stoplight in Washington DC,
        my brother asks me about any girls or guys I've
kissed, as if anyone has to choose sausage or fish,
        one or the other— when the real answer is all,

and I miss the innocent times
when I wasn't uncomfortable at stoplights,
when we'd make grilled cheeses together:
butter the pan, take your white bread

add cheddar cheese on top, let it melt
add salt and pepper, flip the sandwich,
and wow it's ready, with a side of ketchup
on the plate: dip your cheesy bread in,

and now I wonder what century he's living in,
        but I'm the one recalling my mother's stories
about the fortune teller: how my brother will
        end up with a doctor and how I will end up
with a handsome guy, and as I drink more
        Tsingtao, I think about my own lover, who's worried
I'm only dating him for the sake of dating what daddy
        hates, but I tell him over the phone, *No, I date what's sexy.*

Recipe for Lover #4

When my friend, *F* reads my palms, I'm alarmed
        when he tells me that I'll have five great loves
in my life, if the five lines underneath my left
        pinky are any indication, and I think, well,
That's one lover too many, and I can't handle
        this Justice League of my hands, and which one
ends up being my Wonder Woman, the winner
        of it all, the MVP lassoing me towards him—

how Hunk of the Year becomes Hunk of a Lifetime,
        if mangeants are still a thing, and just imagine abs
spray tanned across the runway, because you've got
        to admit that there's something about a man who can
master his runway walk, sashaying away, butt cheeks
        exposed, taking that crown home to me, donning
an apron and cooking me some ramen, add in egg
        and corn and seaweed, and in this landscape

of the couple's palace of tomorrow, I worry
        about the state of my current lover, the way
my hands fit so perfectly on his broad shoulders,
        down onto his back, the way I worry this won't
be forever, because as *F* says, and we all know,
        it usually doesn't work out, the way I wonder
if I could ever love a man who hates tofu,
        unless it's extra firm and burnt to the crisp,

which makes no sense at all, because isn't hating tofu
        like hating bread or rice or cheese or wine or fried
anything, and am I even still a Chinese woman
        if my partner hates tofu, and in bed, I think
about all the recipes we'd be missing out on,
        going out for burgers instead—tasty but standard.
But what about my mother's Cantonese tofu
        and tomatoes dish from my childhood:

Brown the tofu on both sides.
Take two or three fresh tomatoes,
and add in oil and water. Cook
for 10-15 minutes for a boil down,

then the secret ingredient: a dollop
of ketchup. Mix cornstarch with water,
mix it well. Then add in soy sauce
in the pan, some green onion on top.

Oh, how I loved waking up to my mother
        cooking this dish, at eight, and at dinner I'd add
tomatoes atop rice. Now, in bed, my lover
        describes how he can't handle the texture
of tofu, the way he doesn't want that kind
        of party in his mouth, and I know he'd take
that mangeant trophy home, do almost anything
        for me—so why can't he just process the soy.

Triple Sonnet for Hers and Hers Towels and Princess Aurora's Blue/Pink Gown

My brother's wife gifts me a his and hers
          hot chocolate set for Christmas, and I want
to scream, because in what universe are
          his and hers towels and his and hers mugs
and his and hers bathrobes still a thing?
          All I see is his and hers *rubbing it in*
that I don't have a his (that they know of),
          but really, what's with shoving this hetero
agenda down my throat, along with cocoa,
          and my friend Drew says at least I get double
the chocolate, when what I really want is
          a frozen hot chocolate with extra whipped
cream and chocolate shavings and cherry
          on top from Serendipity 3, which is ironic

because that's the site of all the romantic
comedies I hate. And what's with shoving
          the hetero agenda down the throats of young
women, and I remember having a freak out
          at the Krispy Kreme in Rainbow Springs
Shopping Center in Vegas, because if
          gender reveal cakes and gender reveal parties
anger me to no end, then gender reveal donuts
          are the spawn of evil dessert we don't need,
because who chews into a custard crème,
          sees pink or blue, and feels normal afterwards,
when yellow was just fine? It's the economy
          of it all I hate the most—the way blue boy
and pink girl keeps getting pushed, when

the only blue boy I know is the oil portrait
          by Gainsborough or the men's magazine of
abs abs abs and then some more dessert.
          Or what about pink girl / blue girl, also
known as Aurora's color-changing gown

in *Sleeping Beauty,* and it's funny how
this princess only had eighteen minutes
               of screen time, most of which is taken up
by this pink and blue debate, when I really
               wanted to see her in green dancing in
the woods, seducing all the birds around
               her, barefoot, in charge, dumping Prince Phillip,
because that kiss was dry as hell, and a princess
               needs at least sixty minutes of screen time.

Sex Stories and Food

All my sex stories always start off
        with what we ate for dinner,
    and of course, I remember that fancy
            Dragon Roll in Phoenix, Arizona
that lit up on my birthday, and no,
      I usually wouldn't order something so Americanized,
        but the damn thing lit up, a fire-breathing
dragon for a hungry Chinese girl at her birthday party,
     and if you want fun, always add a little fire,

        and my order's usually fresh nigiri all the way,
and I've watched videos on how the California Roll
           was invented, and it's so Cali, so surf culture
with its avocado right in the middle, and I think it's sad
     that most versions don't actually come
        with crab meat, and I think about images of women
in the movies, letting their lovers eat sushi right off
           their bodies, and I wonder if I would ever pull
such a stunt, and he tells me on the phone that he likes me
     in red lipstick, which is a relief, because most men are afraid
      of getting a little messy all over their cheeks
and bodies, but think about how endearing it is in cartoons
      when Minnie is so excited to see Mickey that she gifts him
   red kiss marks all over his cheeks, and you've got to admit
     that everyone has a soft spot for that,

   and instead of sushi all over my body,
I'd rather straight up feed my man some
        fatty tuna, wash it down with cold sake,
spoil him a little, then take charge, then let him
     take charge, back and forth, and for a good time,
       call me, but I'm warning you: I'll be talking
about the food rather than the sex,

because I'm such a tease,
and yes, I've been called that term a million times,
as if I owe anyone *anything* in this world,
and I remember the 4 AM French fries after
the midnight fishbowls full of Blue Curacao and assorted
alcohols and plastic animal toys, and here's a tiger,
here's a cow, here's a dinosaur, meaning here's
my father represented in the Chinese Zodiac,
here's a farm animal, and here's prehistoric times,
in one toy, and do you ever wonder
what a prehistoric times restaurant
would be like, because we already have Medieval Times,
and who doesn't love dinosaurs, and think about
those large plates and plates of turkey legs
or how about Jell-O eggs for dessert,
and I love a little childlike whimsy, and
I love saving hotel room keys for a little sentimental value, remembering
those afternoons spent in a dreamboat's arms,
a couple of laughs, and I always laugh, remember
the room number, what happened in the elevator
on the way back, looking back, and it's like when I collected

Happy Meal toys as a kid, and as a kid,
I loved the scene in *The Phantom Tollbooth*

when the characters deliver speeches
at dinner, listing their favorite foods,

only to be served those exact foods, and I always think
about what my lineup would be: Lobster Ravioli and Lobster Wellington
and Peking Duck and of course, loaded desserts with
lychee and longan and cherries and a couple slices of
grapefruit cake with grapefruit drizzle and poached pears
and peaches, and I told you that I'd rather talk

about the food than the sex, and let's go *around* the subject,
because I'm a tease. I'm a tease. I'm a tease.

Hypersexual

A few years ago, a friend from college married a sex toys heiress in Disneyland.

Years ago, he and I visited Tokyo. Years ago, we lived in Roppongi Hills for five days, slurping ramen in corner shops at night. Years ago, I was nineteen eating the best gyoza of my life. Years ago, he and I pretended to be married for five days in Tokyo. Years ago, five days felt like five minutes. Years ago, I was nineteen. Years ago, he bought me matcha ice cream after a night at the bondage club—the juxtaposition of girls in kitty masks holding my not-my-man-don't-you-want-to-stroke-him-I'll-stroke-you-girl-I'm-not-the   Mrs.-and-I'm-not-in-college-for-the-MRS.-degree-I'm-too-smart-or-not-smart-enough-for-that-goddamnyou, and the girls singing songs making my matcha ice cream concoction at Baskin Robbins will always be on my mind—and then the juxtaposition adds in—the bento we ate the next day at the conference with the miniature hot dogs. At nineteen, I didn't know how to handle hypersexuality in a city of sensory overload to the max. Him in the sauna. Him in a robe. Us married. The girls at the bondage club in kitty masks in our *not couples' fantasy*—I think about stroking her leg then my *not husband's a lot,* even today. He got married in Disneyland to a sex toys heiress. But I know where his magic really happened.

Recipe for Teen Dramas

Because I'm approaching thirty, I can finally star
in a teen drama on primetime TV, and give me that
        longing look and designer wardrobe and that can-do
attitude of a heartthrob who doesn't belong in such
        a small town, and Dear Casting, let me play this useless
main character, your designated hero, the central romantic
        plot, because can that finally be an Asian girl's job?
But my storyline and love life are never useless,

        and I'm telling you: I was born for top billing,
also known as your teen-idol-hottie-protagonist
        who gets into an affair with the sexy teacher
in episode one, but by episode seven, everything
        goes back to normal, like how in children's books,
our protagonists enter the wardrobe or the tollbooth
        or the map or the treasure chest and years and years
and years go by in this alternate timeline, whereas back

        in real life, only minutes have passed, and I think
about my own love life, and how I've got the taste
        for older men: silver foxes who buy me cocktails
and shower me with dinners, and let's watch classic
        cinema together, and that's the typical young and stupid
mistake to make, how years ago, I thought I'd just call it
        a day and marry a rich stud of a man of salt-and-pepper
hair, but those only exist in fairytales, but what if I'm trapped

in all of this fantasy that turns itself on its head,
the way some men want to pay for ten more minutes
        of a young Asian woman's time, and you bet your ass,
if I was on a teen drama, I'd play the central character
        who starts an affair with the hot teacher, and in real life,
these men will never understand me, because they're only
        as good as the food on the table lasts, and they don't
get why I need to keep a little Hong Kong in me:

                        and growing up, I'd eat chicken wings,
                        Cantonese style in front of the television:
                        Sauté your chicken wings with two tablespoons
                        of oil until golden. Add in ginger, spring onion,
                        and parsley, and fry for a little. Add in your sauce:
                        half a teaspoon of sugar, a pinch pepper, a dash
                        of sesame oil, half a tablespoon of wine, half
                        a tablespoon of light soy, half a cup of water,

                        half a teaspoon of chicken powder,
                        and add in that sauce. Then arrange your wings
                        in the wok, cover and boil. Bake over low heat
                        for five minutes. Add in oyster sauce, then stir
                        and bake for just a little. Add in corn flour mix
                        with water for thickening. Dish up. Discard
                        your ginger, spring onion, and parsley.
                        Serve and enjoy. Watch your primetime soap.

        And I want to star in a teen drama because I can
be forever young and stupid with no consequences,
        and isn't that the dream—give me today and tomorrow
and the fountain of youth at the end of the day when I leave
        my silver fox, eat dinner alone, and onto episode seven,
back to normal teenage life of boys and girls and bowling
        and milkshakes and cars and what even happens on
the season finale—don't leave me on a cliffhanger, baby.

Recipe for Teen Dramas 2

Of course, there's a season 2. I'm a baby-faced girl
approaching thirty, which means I can finally star
        in a teen drama on primetime TV, and in the cliffhanger
continued that opens the season, my character is caught
        with another older man, but by episode five, we forget
about him completely, and you served your purpose, buddy—
        good day, and give me that unlimited wardrobe that gets
more risqué each season and a plotline that forever *kills*,

        and let's talk about romance, or that moment when
our teen-idol-hottie-protagonists bump uglies for
        the first time in the back of a moving vehicle, but
oh wait, that's my fantasy come to life, and always
        use protection, kids. But let's talk about romance
and how our lives are centered around it, like romance
        exists as the designer drug we just can't live without,
and isn't it *romantic* how many darkhorses on teen dramas

        are writers dating the hottest girl in school, and she's his
forever muse in this world of milkshakes and drive-in
        makeouts and junior proms, and oh, that moment of
discovery when they lose their virginities to each other—
        cue the music, because it's oh so awkward, yet oh so
beautiful, and it's oh so awkward, yet oh so beautiful.
        But I'm not a teenager anymore—I haven't been for
at least a decade, and in my world, everything is flipped,   —

        I realize, when Rita and I are talking about men who
want to be muses, because as Rita says, it's so romantic
        for them to appear in a poem or a dream or a home video,
and they're aiming for leading man status when they're only
        the guest star, and I hate to break it to one in particular—
I just don't have the heart, but this isn't an open casting call,
        boy. The set is now closed, and Rita and I laugh as we're
cooking spring rolls, and there's nothing better than this:

Ingredients: 1/3 lb chicken meat, 2/3 oz black mushrooms,
½ lb silver sprouts, 2 2/3 oz yellow chives, sectioned,
20 spring roll wrappings. Marinade: Dash of sesame oil
and pepper, 1 tbsp light soy sauce, 1/3 tsp salt,
1/3 tsp sugar, ½ tsp mung bean flour, ½ tsbp oil.
Paste for sealing: 1 tsbp plain flour, 2/3 tbsp water:
blend well. Now, wash, wipe, and shred chicken meat.
Marinate for 10 minutes. Soak your black mushrooms

to soften and remove stems. Squeeze out excess water
and steam for 10 minutes. Shred finely. Stir-fry sprouts
with 1 tbsp of oil. Dish. Stir-fry chicken with 2 tbsp of oil
until cooked. Add mushrooms and silver sprouts. Mix and
add in chives. Dish in drainer to drain off excess juice. Wrap
each spring roll wrapping with a portion of filling. Form in rolls
and seal in ends with flour paste. Heat up frying pan with 6 tbsp
of oil. Fry spring rolls over medium low until golden. Dish.

And there's nothing better than this: spring rolls
in front of the TV, and we talk about men who want
        so badly to become muses, and I think back to the grand
tradition of the Odalisque: the perfect curvature of her
        back, the feather, the look right into the camera, and
no boy, this isn't an open casting call, and you're out
        after this week, but why don't you take off your
shirt, roll around for me—that romantic ending.

Recipe for Loneliness

We tell each other about our fantasies over
        the phone, like how he wants me to touch him
under the table at a bar, or how I'd like for us
        to have our way with each other in a moving
vehicle in the middle of the night, and maybe
        the windows should be down, letting us feel
the breeze at 3 AM, and I'll reminisce on simpler
        times of body shots and grinding at clubs—

and we move onto dreams, dirty dreams involving
        each other, and I tell him about the dream I had
the night before, of us locked in a room of glass
        walls, making love in front of a revolving door
of audience members coming in and out, like a mixed
        reviews exhibit at a museum of contemporary art,
and with each new person entering, he enters me
        a little deeper, and I moan a little harder, a little

faster, a little crazier—positive feedback loop, yes,
        eyes rolled behind my head, and I'm such a fan
of modern architecture, but tonight, I wonder if there
        actually is a cure for loneliness, other than finding
someone long distance to pass the time with, maybe
        something a little more, and I think about how
celebrities freak at the sight of all-glass houses,
        their lives on further display, and when I play

simulation games, my avatars always put on a show
        in all-glass rooms, and I think, at heart, we're all
exhibitionists, who want every single grand thing
        this world has to offer, like the Romans with their
Corinthian columns, or what about Renaissance art,
        for instance, Donatello's naked beautiful boy *David*
working it, foot on Goliath's head, and on the phone,
        I'm hungry for this man I share fantasies with, but

for real, I'm also *hungry* for dessert—
something decadent like coconut and sago soup,
and any recipe that calls for coconut milk
is always a winner, so wash and cut
your 2/3 lb. of fresh taro into thick slices,
then steam on a plate for 30 minutes, until
softened. Press to purée. Soak your sago
for about half an hour, then boil two cups

of water. Add in your sago and cook until
it turns transparent. Take a sieve and dip
in cold water, removing any stickiness.
Drain well. Boil 2 ½ cups of water. Add
in sago, sugar, and taro puree. Bring to a boil.
Add in coconut milk (the best part!).
Bring to a boil and pour in evaporated milk.
Mix well. Serve hot or cold. But really, cold.

And I'm hungry for this man I share fantasies with,
     and doesn't a photo just make you crave the real
thing, the real flesh even more, he asks me, and yes,
     that's true, and I picture all the masterpieces of
nude beauties with the softest skin in the world,
     the way it feels so real on canvas, then the way
I wish I could touch him over the phone tonight,
     and oh, I crave and I crave and crave and crave.

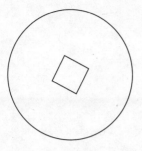

IV.
AN ODE TO
DECADENCE

Psychic Crush of the Week

I have crushes on girls who are psychic,
        because I'm drawn to the beauty of knowing
everything, and it's fun knowing everything,

        isn't it, honey? I see you right there seeing right
through me, and I'll admit I want to be psychic
        too, join you as the Psychic Girl of the Week—

Psychic Girl of Your Dreams, and I wonder if
        the Eastern Zodiac can help me get there—
my Year of the Snake compatible with Oxen

        and Dragons and especially Roosters, and why'd
it have to be the cock, anyway? How overrated,
        and we all know that nothing beats a woman's

touch, a woman's kisses, a woman's neck, and
        my fantasies with women are always much more
elaborate, like piles of pastries in Rococo rooms

        with floral wallpaper and a million camera angles
and a canopy bed as we strip each other—vanilla
        éclairs and opera cakes and raspberry tarts and pink

soufflés and strawberry cream puffs and green apple
        and orange blossom macarons: this erotic fashion
show I once dreamt of when I was a girl pulling up

        lace thigh highs, or the first time I kissed another
woman in my bed, telling her to use less tongue,
        because I wanted more intimacy—less playfulness,

a little more, and studies show that luxury is often
        associated with women, and I think about how in
simulation games, my lead female role *always* falls

        for another woman, and they move into a mansion
filled with Victorian busts and Vanitas still lifes

and human-sized bird cages, mimicking the fantasy

I had last night when my dream and I kissed
        in the antechamber, and she carried me, proceeding
to ask which room I'd love most to make love in,

        and we chose the smallest one, because I liked
the royal blue couch and Tiffany green pillows
        and the peacock feathers all over. And wouldn't it

be funny to make love in a wine cellar or a broom
        closet or a pantry, and let's get a snack in between
sessions, maybe some creamed cookies or cereal

        with marshmallows or something hot and spicy—
I'll feed you if you feed me—but this was all sweet
        dreams last night, and now I think back to college

when my best friend and I wrote porn together:
        characters who could remove their heads, characters
in masks, characters that transformed into mermaids

        in the shower, and centaurs, and monsters from
a more beautiful Earth—everything under the moon
        you could possibly think of, but I never called her again

because we didn't share the same fantasy. I never called
        her again because we didn't share the same fantasy,
and all dreams come to an end, as I wake up, now

        trying to hold onto the lover in the royal blue room
with its exotic plants and clam-shaped chairs, like
        Hollywood starlet makes love to Hollywood starlet,

and look dear, a peacock, a bouquet of hydrangeas,
        a philosopher's bust, a trophy filled with cream puffs,
and a lady centaur storms right in, and I'm kissing you,

        and look, the wallpaper grew an eye, a cheetah dances,
the cabbage roses bloom, and we share a macaron
        as you read my mind—we're never moving out.

Ode to Sitting Courtside at a Lakers Game

       The ideal relationship is courtside at a Lakers Game
chowing on three hotdogs: extra relish and mustard,
         because life is about seeing and being seen, taking me
back to an MTV childhood when Carmen Electra
         was voted Most Pauseworthy Female, and the language
was all wrong, but she was so right in declaring life
         wasn't worth living unless there was a camera around—
how La La Anthony called her a smart girl, and who would

                  ever be in denial. I could be your attention whore, your
           millennial cam girl, your straight no chaser brat, I tell
              a lover on Christmas after he requests a sex tape as
his gift, and I read stories of women showering ahead
              of time, throwing on enough eyeliner and mascara—
the camera trick—the narrative we set in our sex lives—
              we all want to look beautiful on command, but what
about connection. I'm extra wet in bed after that call. V

       is for very very sexy. V is for video burned to
DVD burned to Blu-Ray burned to a streaming
         service near you, and it's strange to live through
more than one decade. V is for verde, the color of
         celebrity kitchens nowadays, and I dream of getting
pounded right on the counter next to a bowl of fruits,
         or how in college, we'd stare at Cezanne and call it
very very sexy attention to detail—these fruits—
         those oranges—that attention to detail, and undress

                  me like a peach because V is the letter Mad Men once
were most afraid of, questioning if women would ever fly
             Virgin Air or buy products that started with letter V,
when we all know now virginity is a social construct,
           and the question isn't *When did she lose her virginity*
but *When did she gain her sexuality* or *When did her
             sexuality come into full play?* It's vulva not vagina that
gives pleasure. According to blonde women, a candle can

smell like a vagina. According to brunette women,
the modifier for le vagine shouldn't be masculine
                but feminine. But I like to be called bro is what
I'd say back. A man tells me I'm not very butch
                after I tell him I'm into feminine women. Vacant.
V is for versatility and serving up some realness.
                Every day is the beauty pageant of the Monopoly
game. V is for vendetta or the comic book you'd draw

    me in, or how kink queen Violet Chachki once said
drag was the art of not looking like a woman but
        a *drawing* of a woman. V is for Vanessa Williams
playing woman Wilhelmina Slater on *Ugly Betty* having
        hot sex with her hunk of a bodyguard right before
her wedding to the old white man. If you were sitting
        courtside at the Lakers would your bodyguard block
everyone else's view? I sure hope not. Pass me a hotdog.

Carmen Electra Once Said

"Life is not worth living unless there's a camera around—for me."

I remember how an MTV News reporter called her a smart girl, because let's face it: she's the superhero origin story of legends, or the starlet rising out of the clam shell, or remember Debbie Reynolds jumping out of the cake to a delighted Gene Kelly in *Singin' in the Rain*,

and I dream of her too, like Venus in Botticelli, transforming from Tara Leigh Patrick to

Carmen Electra,

A name that sounds like lighting blue—lighting in a bottle—or the entire dessert menu.

Delicious is a word a lover calls me: "You're so fucking delicious" and "You're just so yummy," and we devour reach other.

I remember the scene during Electra's seven-episode reality show, *Til Death Do Us Part,* when Carmen and her then-husband Dave Navarro, taste wedding cakes. What a predicament to choose between

Sweet, classic All-American vanilla and elegant, British-inspired and layered with toffee

Or was that a dig into sexual politics? All I know is that on *Desperate Housewives,* the two cakes were a metaphor for Susan Mayer's white woman predicament of choosing between two men. My response? Try polyamory, Susan.

Besides, Gaby Solis was the real star of that show. And who could forget Bree Van de Kamp truly serving *housewife* with her pies and frittatas and scones and of course, the muffins, the Sunday night show of the early aughts, inspired by *American Beauty,* that led to a reality television franchise, only it's a dead woman, rather than a dead man who narrates.

And for the record, Dave Navarro preferred Ho Hos over any fancy cakes. I forget what Carmen preferred. I was too busy pausing the screen.
                              Why are goddesses so fleeting?

Carmen's overlined eyes in the early 2000s—how makeup teaches us to emphasize our best features, and will you take a photo of me in bisexual lighting—
                    I want to repeat my girlhood discoveries.

34D

Like the apartment number you memorize. Like your favorite item on the lunch menu. Like your choice in the vending machine: Pizza Combos OR salt and vinegar chips OR Tropical Skittles. Or I'm thirsty for a Cherry Coke. Hand over your cash. A Cherry Coke over my breast. An older man once said, "Your poetry is like Frank O'Hara's....only sexier." I took this as compliment. I'm not sure how to feel now.... I hate ellipsis.... they're too much unearned suspense. A Cherry Coke with vanilla ice cream to share. Two cherries = a double scoop. A double dish. The painting with the twin cherries wearing panties. The dish would like to order two dishes: Lobster Stuffed Salmon AND Linguini with Clams. Twin cherries, as in the slot machine I played with at the age of ten before security scolded me. 34D as in Victoria's secret compartment. 34D as in Victoria's transphobic, so stop paying her. Her secrets are basic and boring. 34D as in bedazzle my bra. D as in the almost failing grade—but who's the teacher—I petition for an A. I'll do my extra credit. Make it a plus. 34D as in Goddess Bless Wilhemina Slater on *Ugly Betty* for using her measurements as her safe combination. Lock and key. Show off your assets. 34D as in coverage but take it off. 34D as in I'll cover the roaming costs. 34D as in the wandering eyes. 34D as in as in as in what does sex have to do with poetry. Everything and nothing.

Ode, if Your Love Language is Physical Touch

When men and women say they like the things I like,
        like Caravaggio and the stars, I want them to shut up,
because it's not a pick-up line if we're all looking
        at the same sky every night, and make a wish,
honey, because it's not a come-on, or a turn-on,
        or a turn me on against the wall at a museum
in the middle of the day as tourists watch, and oh,
        go a little harder—*just* a little harder, and boys
and girls and girls and girls and boys and boys
        meet in front of masterpieces, falling in love,
and we all know the endings of those stories,
        but have you seen Caravaggio's painting of the four
musician boys—all identical, almost unclothed,
        porcelain skin, string that mandolin, and have you
ever been so infatuated with someone you wished
        upon a genie that they'd quadruple right before
your eyes dressing and undressing in a montage
        out of an '80s film starring Anthony Michael Hall,
and yes, it's a little greedy—a little barbaric,
        Barbarella stripping in space—to want four of
the same person, but isn't it lovely to have four
        times the flesh, the skin on your hands, massaging
their back down to their butt, I think, one night
        when I'm figuring out which of the five love
languages I am, and all I want is physical touch,
        because it's existed since the Stone Age—all chemistry
and dynasty and history, and let your man serve you,
        every night, or as my lover whispers, "My pleasure"
to me on the phone, a voice that makes me want
        to be a little barbaric, a little Barbarella, naked
in space—what a babe, make love to him in
        zero gravity, which is such a Double 007 move,
plus the martinis with extra olives plus the gadgets
        in the bedroom, and touch me, light my fire, baby,
and we'll light a fire here, paint some animals on

the wall like our ancestors, and oh, you've got me
going so hard, you've got me going so hard,
        paint on my hands, markings left after you
bring me down to this earth—into your arms—
        into this zero-gravity space of just you and me—all
I need is your physical touch with a side of olives.

Ode to Role Play

Once Upon a Time in Singapore,
   an architect tells me I look like a porn star
with my thick-rimmed Tom Ford glasses,
   like a good girl caught in the middle of
the act, holding a dirty martini.

      Once Upon a Time in Greek Mythology,
    Aphrodite marries Hephaestus over Poseidon
      and Ares, because he promises that she'll
   never have to work a day in her life. She kisses
      him, water dripping off her perfect nude body.

Once Upon a Time on Lover's Lane,
   a romantic lead tells me he wants schoolgirl
roleplay, because that's the sexual answer
   when your girl's a professor. Lecturing is sexy,
he says. He gets rewarded—an A+ for logic.

      Once Upon a Time on Wisteria Lane, Gabrielle
    Solis is almost caught with her gardener after
      he leaves a gym sock under the bed. She convinces
   her husband it's the maid's. Episodes later, Lynette's
      the one wearing the maid outfit, trying to seduce.

Once Upon a Time on the Internet,
   G laughs over how I call my lovers "love interests,"
like "you're a casting director," she says.
   I've got an eye for talent. I eye the talent. I want
two eyes tattooed to my nape to watch everyone.

Once Upon a Time in Toon Town, Jessica Rabbit
tells Roger she'll bake him a carrot cake. She loves
a toon who makes her laugh—her raspy voice—
my animated crush forever. One night my own crush
wonders if anyone's ever crushed on Roger himself.

Once Upon a Time in the Sext Chain,
I send him photos of me undressing, after
donning a red gingham apron top. I could
bend over, bake a cherry pie. We depict sexiness
as cherries, peaches, and flames over Emoji.

Once Upon a Time in Long Distance Land,
he tells me that getting tattooed feels like
getting a hard paddling. I remember stumbling into
sex shops at twenty, touching teddy bear shaped
paddles, because I can be a little sweet, too.

Once Upon a Time in a Fairy Tale, a Princess
opens her nudes by accident in the middle of
a café. A couple sits behind her. Every sexual
act advances the plot in some way. After all, it's
much better to play and prance in your displays.

Triple Sonnet for Losing My Virginity Again

I dream of losing my virginity again
        in Singapore when I'm in a deep sleep
on a queen bed with fluffed pillows
        and white sheets—*Good night, Dorothy.*
And sometimes in life, I feel like a virgin,
        because my ears aren't pierced, no tattoos—
aren't I such a nice girl for you to take home
        to Mommy? Let me bake cookies for her,
messing up in pigtails and a frilly apron
        in the kitchen, while the intercom yells,
Baking is a science, or some other gibberish
        I don't care for—I'm such a nice, wholesome
girl licking the batter, and cookie dough's
        the best topping for brownies and ice cream,

        and I flash you on the countertop, a pink thong
exposing my butt cheeks, straight out of your
        pornographic memory, straight out of a home
video—press play, lick my cake, press play,
        lick my cake—go ahead and lick whipped cream
off my nipples, off my chest, and I dream
        of losing my virginity again in deep sleep
in Singapore, but now I'm transported to
        an office, sitting on an office chair, answering
office emails, and an office man opens the door,
        and he's got the same face as a man I knew
from college. I get up, stroke his hair, tell him
        to sit down, and I want him to enter me, oh
so badly, and he enters me right then and there

on the office chair, my pink panties tossed
        aside, and I moan in pain, I moan in pleasure,
but isn't that so cliché, reading like romance
        novels, or remember in the early 2000s
modeling competitions when girls faced off

with looks serving Harlequin covers—look,
she's a milkmaid and he's a farmhand. Look,

    she's a poor girl and he's from the upper crust,
and back in the office, I moan more, then wake

    in Singapore on a white bed with fluffed pillows,
and I feel pain. I feel like I'm bleeding, only

    there's no blood. I think about my double loss
of stupidity and how no pain will ever top

    the pain I feel right now as I'm awakened again.

Triple Sonnet for Batman Villains and Whatever This Is

I want to judge a shirtless contest in Vegas
        poolside with my best friend, over Mai Tais
and shrimp tacos, because I'm a little sapphic,
        and let me just say: Cheers to our BDE forever,
girl. We're like 007's Bambi and Thumper,
        only undefeated, and in this fantasy, we'll keep
kicking Sean Connery's *Diamonds Are Forever*
        ass, or how Tommy Lee Jones' Two-Face in
Batman Forever was the luckiest man alive,
        with Sugar and Spice cooking him lemon souffle,
quail eggs, and poached salmon, and all the meats
        and heat—meats and heat, but what woman even
needs a man. Or men. Let's prance around in
        white feathered robes, and cheers to Drew Barrymore

        giving us sexy '90s villain fantasy, and how many
rappers will write songs about you in a lifetime
        is a question for only a legend. And I'm a little
sapphic, thinking about my first crushes on women,
        or how Taneum says that it's stupid when people
call them "girl crushes" when we know they're
        crushes—or maybe even true love, the idea that
we could be dripping in diamonds together, but
        you're just playing. I could play too. Let's go out
for sushi—a love boat filled with sashimi and Snow
        Beauty sake and mango mochi for dessert. I often
think about Harley Quinn and Poison Ivy sharing
        a Christmas tree and one-bedroom apartment in
Gotham, and it's beautiful how in recent timelines,

Harley doesn't go back to Mister J. Not all women
        want men in their lives. I remember Barbara asking
me what all these guys were doing in my poems.
        I don't know, B. I really don't know. Or how
one night, a lover asks about the first woman

who loved me, L—how back in college we would
nap together naked and keep kissing until the sun set,
     and then I'd walk home wearing her flannel after
she redid my lipstick. Sometimes when I'm down,
     I search for that girl, walking home in the dark—
how at that age, I knew I'd take over the world,
     how at that age, I knew I'd never settle, because
there are too many fish in the sea. I still am that girl,
     swimming, searching—guided by the Ithaca moon.

V.
ONE MORE DESSERT FOR DISCOVERY

Ode to Petaloso

Over drinks, my friend Giulio is telling me about this great new Italian word,
    petaloso, coined by a child to describe that moment you look at a flower and feel
intense happiness, *petaloso,* because it's so beautiful with all its petals,
    and isn't it priceless, like that moment you're having a really great orgasm,
and the heavens and angels descend upon you, as your lover possesses
    that special ability to make you come without removing a single article
of clothing, just by sucking right below the collar bone, also known
    as the sexiest part of a woman, and dab on some highlighter there, girls,
because sometimes, just sometimes, life on Earth really isn't that bad,
    and the orgasm ends up bringing a Renaissance painting to life,
and if you ask me, I'd prefer a masterpiece from the Mannerist era—
    think Bronzino's *Venus, Cupid, Folly, and Time,* where such a great time's
had by Venus and Cupid that they momentarily forget they're mother and son,
    and look, Venus holds that golden apple from Paris,
because we are women and we use our feminine wiles and we conquer all
    and we eat all and conquer and eat and conquer, eat and conquer
as Father Time, *daddy,* tries to get in on the fun, behind the curtain,
    petaloso, because you're so happy that time and space and dimension
blend together, and where are we again? And back on Earth, girlfriend,
    we order another round, a couple Amaros now, and Giulio is telling me
about his pet tortoise back in Naples, who hibernates most of the year
    and loves tomatoes, and I think petaloso, because how charming,
and how tomatoes remind me of my mother who cooks
    chicken wings dipped in a Cantonese tomato sauce, with scallions,
and her tofu dishes that use that same sauce, and tomatoes,
    because when I was in high school, my parents and I visited
an Andy Warhol exhibit, so I think about those Campbell's Soup cans
    and Marilyn and Elizabeth and Grace and those sunrises
and sunsets, and oh, keep me happy, and did you know that the word
    for pistachio in Cantonese is literally translated as "happy nut,"
because it forms a smile, and again, *petaloso,* as our steak frites arrive and we order
    more food, and *petaloso,* everything's so delicious
I feel a million petals forming in my stomach and heart and brain,
    and out of this world into a painting, there's my signature in the corner.

Triple Sonnet for Studmuffins Wrapped in Bacon

I'd like to order a lover wrapped in bacon
        from your secret menu, because I'm a really
hungry Chinese girl at this drive-in—
        give me all meat, all man, 100% Grade A
all-natural cut with a side of sensitive,
        and don't forget the condiments in the bag,
and isn't this ideal? Having your cake
        and eating it too, or having your beefcake
and eating *him* too, or having your studmuffin
        feed you strawberry cake in the bubble bath
like you're both rich and happy with unlimited
        wardrobes and private jets, and I want to feel
like women with enviable thighs, in erotica
        winding up their men: she winds, he drools,

        she winds, he drools—her boy toy or man toy,
and I want to lean in for a kiss after telling
        my lover about wrapping *him* in bacon,
because bacon tastes good on everything
        from deviled eggs to mac and cheese,
and Heart Attack Burgers on secret menus:
        three greasy patties and bacon bacon bacon,
a little melted cheese, and once I watched
        an interview with a starlet who said how
melted cheese was her favorite food,
        and no more beautiful words have ever
been spoken, and let food be your fantasy:
        how children believe that the moon is made
of cheese or how adults want to live in houses

made of gouda, and in Hong Kong, my cousin
        Janet recommends cheese hot pot with chicken,
and no, that's not the same thing as fondue
        also known as the 2000s version of romantic:
dip your date in cheese, or take me back

to the drive-in, and let me order some #1s
of hunks of men on bread dipped in cheese
        and some #4s of man sandwiches: cut
and chiseled to perfection with tomatoes
        and special sauce, or what about some #5s
on the breakfast menu: studmuffins both sweet
        and full of whole grains and buff buff buff,
and why is it that I start giggling when my love
        and I start talking about food—pass the sauce,

        please, I'm ready to eat you up, order you again.

Triple Sonnet, Because Boy, You're Starstruck and I'm a Wonder

Boy, you're starstruck. I love the way you rub
        the red lipstick off above my Cupid's bow—
how you call it the halo of my face, because
        girliness equals goodness equals godliness
equals, let's be real, *Oh My Goddess*, like that
        moment when Hades and Persephone meet
in the fractured Greek myth, and the Goddess
        of Spring chugs her can of pomegranate soda,
because her future lover is oh so fine, and check
        out that ass. They don't make stories like this
anymore, do they? Boy, you're my good afternoon
        delight as the Fountains at the Bellagio go off,
as the tourists at the bistro across the street
        munch on Steak Béarnise and Croque Monsieur

        and Wild Escargots de Bourgogne, as the water
dances to Sinatra's *Come Fly with Me,*
        and I've just about named every cliché
in the romance book, minus the flowers—
        I had to stuff the Vegas Strip in there, but no,
let me start over now. *F* was right that day
        in Tallahassee when he traced the lines on
my palm and said the three long ones at the end
        meant I'd have many great loves in my life,
and how I laughed at *F*'s face after. And oh, Boy,
        was *F* right, I think, when *X* asks me on the phone
if I've ever been in love, and I say *No* too fast,
        and I might be lying to her, but who really
cares? I used to want to outsex everyone, make

everyone want, make everyone pant,
        make everyone chew their steak just a little
harder, order that extra shot of whiskey.
        And his lips go wild because I've just drank
bourbon—that extra tingle of tongue—

the red lipstick that gets him all messy,
gets me all messy again, gives me the halo
        above my Cupid's bow, and what's it like
being in lust with a man and a woman
        at the same time—it's like dancing in a corner,
your tank top about to slip off, exposing
        nipples, but you keep dancing. And Boy,
I'm a wonder, and when you kiss me,
        I think about *her* red lips kissing me.

Comet and Cupid

I wonder what it's like being *actually* in love.

I put on a silk chemise and call him—the room is fuchsia tonight. I tell him I am nonbinary. All I get is love—amore—tender, like Kobe beef in hotpot—我愛你—Ngo5 Oi3 Nei5, let me speak Cantonese to you—that moment when the snow falls on the tip of your nose at the start of winter—in return.

I tell him I'm now she/they. People at work keep asking if it's "she" or "they" when it's both and all. World, will you switch it up and shut up and listen. He says I need to get out of this town. I wonder what it's like being *actually* in love. He tells me about his fantasies: us in the same city, us kissing under my desk—*We can keep each other warm even without sheets.* I think so too.

Every time he laughs, his face carries the extra grin. I tell him every poem has a volta.

Taneum tells me about comets, or lovers who pass through your life for joy in its most distilled form. When I was a kid in the nineties, I thought I'd take over the world. That train hasn't passed.

The Love Potion No. Whatever cocktail in this town is made from

Yeoman Wheat Vodka
Spiced Pear Liquor
Lemon Juice
Brown Sugar
Syrup
Cranberry Juice
Rosemary

He tells me I need to get out of this town. I wonder what it's like for a she/they Chinese femme who will take over the world, to *actually* be in love. We talk about Marquez. Magical Realism. The sensual dishes in *Dona Flor and Her Two Husbands*: marinated crab, vatapá, and corn cake. Guillermo del toro characters. The way nuance in film is sexy. I wish I could be in Dona Flor's class while she's chopping the onions and putting in the tomatoes.

I sit on my doorstep in 50-degree weather late at night. A comet flies by every decade. Comet is my favorite reindeer. Periodic to every day is the transformation of my own comet. I drink cumin mixed with vanilla mixed with ginger mixed with cinnamon mixed with hot milk. When I was a kid, the teacher assigned me to be Aphrodite in a play. I wonder what it's like being *actually* in love.

Triple Sonnet for Snakes Eating Cocks

Do cocks and snakes get along, I wonder,
        when I know the answer is *yes, yes,* and more
yes, when my lover and I get in trouble
        for kissing at the bar, and I want to tell you
I'm scared this is going to be a love story.
        This *is* a love story, where we see each other
once a year, and the waiter interrupts us to
        "Keep it PG," but since when is living about
keeping your tongue out of the subject of your
        affection's mouth? Since when is living not
about taking that gulp of bourbon, spilling it
        on your breast? Since when is living not about
following luck and intuition and ambition,
        and *Hello, Fortune. Hello, Boy.* Did you know

        snakes and cocks are a match of complements,
and *yes,* we kiss for hours. We talk for days.
        Explaining the Chinese Zodiac to you is like
explaining my childhood to a lover, the way
        I grew up in the Pennsylvania suburbs, eating
hotpot with my parents—make it extra spicy:
        add in bok choy and enoki and fish balls and scallops
and prawns with their heads intact, and beef balls
        for the dog, and *Hello, Boy,* I'm like Christmas
morning to you, the seduction of the zodiac—
        you wrap your leg around mine, and I love
the way you smell, and right now, you need
        to know that a Snake Woman will always get
what she wants, swallow you whole. And Dear

Rooster, Dear Cock, Dear Boy, run away now
        if you can't handle it—if you can't handle me,
because being with a snake woman is like
        being trapped in a glass cage with no way out.
And Christmas morning for me, growing up,

was visiting Chinatown with my Rabbit
Mother and Tiger Father, buying egg tarts,
        buying red envelopes, buying coconut mochi,
buying fortune telling books for the year ahead,
        and did you know that people born under
the Year of the Rooster are destined to either
        be great writers or ordinary human beings?
So, which one are you? Which one will you be
        for me? I think we could be beautiful—I think.

VERSIONS OF THESE POEMS HAVE APPEARED OR ARE FORTHCOMING IN THE FOLLOWING JOURNALS AND ANTHOLOGIES:

The Account. "Triple Sonnet and Three Cheers for the Asian Bachelorette" and "Triple Sonnet for Hers and Hers Towels and Princess Aurora's Blue/Pink Gown."

Asian American Writer's Workshop, The Margins. "Triple Sonnet for Dennis Rodman, #91, on my Television Screen."

The Boiler. "Triple Sonnet for Losing My Virginity Again"

The Cincinnati Review. "So Chinese Girl."

The Cincinnati Review—miCRO Series. "34D."

Colorado Review. "Triple Sonnet for Batman Villains and Whatever This Is."

Denver Quarterly. "Ode to Heavy Appetizers and Many Big Loves."

Dreginald. "Ode to Lasagna," "Triple Sonnet for Silver Foxes, Dear Dad, and Alex Trebek, Teach Me Something Actually Useful," "Triple Sonnet for Snakes Eating Cocks," and "Triple Sonnet for Asian Girlfriends: Cancel My Membership."

Figure 1. "Recipe for Loneliness."

Gettysburg Review. "Designer" and "Designer."

HAD. "Triple Sonnet for Veronica Lodge's Tigers."

Juked. "Sex Stories and Food."

Ki Online. "Designer."

The McNeese Review: Boudin. "Recipe for Teen Dramas."

The Offing. "Triple Sonnet for Dragons Spitting Out Pearls."

Oyez Review. "Recipe for Teen Dramas 2."

Palette Poetry. "Chinese Girl Strikes Back."

Passages North. "Psychic Crush of the Week."

POETRY Magazine. "Triple Sonnet for Black Hair," "Ode to Chinese Superstitions, Haircuts, and Being a Girl," "Triple Sonnet, Because Boy, You're Starstruck and I'm a Wonder," and "Triple Sonnet for Celebrities with Three Names."

Poets.org. Academy of American Poets. "So Chinese Girl."

Redivider. "Ode to Petaloso."

Superstition Review. "Ode to Sitting Courtside at a Lakers Game."

Verse Daily. "Triple Sonnet for Batman Villains and Whatever This Is."

Washington Square Review. "I'm the Sad Girl in the Anime Masturbating."

WHERE ELSE. An International Hong Kong Poetry Anthology. "Triple Sonnet for Veronica Lodge's Tigers."

Waxwing. "Triple Sonnet for Corn Soup," "Triple Sonnet for Studmuffins Wrapped in Bacon," "Recipe for Rudeness," "Recipe for Lover #4," and "Ode, if Your Love Language is Physical Touch."

ACKNOWLEDGEMENTS

For Rita Mookerjee—"The lake looks the bluest when / your best friend is your life partner and soul / mate." And to many more years of Honey Literary Inc. and doing life together.

For Sebastián H. Páramo—Cheers to many more years of doing poetry together. Thank you for believing in me. Nordstrom forever.

For Rosebud Ben-Oni—In every universe.

For Justin Greene—Brazil, Hong Kong, New York, Tampa.

For Phil Spotswood—Airports and train stations aren't just about destinations but also arrivals. You are home.

For Daniel Peña—Go Big Red.

For Taneum Bambrick—Thank you for finding me in Tampa. I will never let go.

For Andrew Yellow Bird—IHOP at 2 AM in Phoenix, AZ, is the start to every poem.

For Jessica Q. Stark—I live for your laugh every AWP. AB for life.

For Sakinah Hofler—I will always remember that day in the graduate student work room.

For Yvel Clovis—Poetic lines are like camera angles.

For Elissa Hutson—Calmness is a superpower. Cheers to the smell of pine. Cheers to instinct.

For Alan Chazaro— To liquid courage. To understanding the aesthetics of basketball. To anime GIFs. To finding a poetry sibling at the right time. Right here. Right now.

For Gustavo Hernandez—"If you fucked god, would you call the next day?" Yes is the sexiest word in the English language besides etc.

For Christina Giarrusso—Cheers to our biannual Honey Literary ritual. It's so special.

For Lyrae Van Clief-Stefanon—The sonnet is the infinite amuse-bouche. Thank you for being my lifelong friend and mentor. Boy, was I lucky to meet you when I was nineteen and clueless about the world and poetry.

For Richard Siken—Thank you for starting it.

For Mom + Dad—Love is infinite. I will always make you proud.

For Grandpa + in loving memory of Grandma—I will always write a poem about the eels in the tank for you.

In loving memory of the one and only Norman Dubie. I miss you every day. I do not know who I would have become without you.

In loving memory of the legendary Michael Koch. I wish we could get soup at the Temple of Zeus one last time.

Thank you to all my mentors. Seriously, thank you for putting up with me. And more seriously, thank you for teaching me generosity: Alice Fulton, Alberto Ríos, Dennis Moore and Dear Barbara, Stephanie Vaughn, Joanie Mackowski, and Jeannine Savard.

Thank you to Patty Paine, Law Alsobrook, and Zoë Shankle Donald for your kindness over the years.

Thank you to my dear friends: Mickey Singer, Yena Kim, Misha Rai, Antony Fangary, Keith S. Wilson, Stephanie Tom, Jenny Molberg, Nabila Lovelace, Diamond Forde, K. Iver, Adam Silverstein, Kendra Bartell, Dustin Pearson, Dean Guo, Diwakar Gupta, and Anna Kortright.

Thank you to the Honey Hive. Why is our masthead so objectively hot.

Thank you to Joshua David Watson and Jordan Nakamura for that fun day in LA.

A million thank yous to everyone at Deep Vellum: Will Evans, Sara Balabanlilar, Walker Rutter-Bowman, and Linda Stack-Nelson.

Photo credit: Joshua David Watson